THiS bOOK bELONGS tO

Isla

Published 2016 by Bloomsbury Publishing Plc
50 Bedford Square, London, WC1B 3DP

www.bloomsbury.com

Bloomsbury is a registered trademark of Bloomsbury Publishing Plc

978 1 4088 8367 9

Insides produced by Frilly Fish Books

A CIP record for this book is available from the British Library.

Printed in China by Leo Paper Products

This book is produced using paper that is made from wood
grown in managed, sustainable forests. It is natural, renewable
and recyclable. The logging and manufacturing processes conform
to the environmental regulations of the country of origin.

1 3 5 7 9 10 8 6 4 2

MY LOVELY CHRISTMAS BOOK

BLOOMSBURY

LONDON OXFORD NEW DELHI NEW YORK SYDNEY

Photo

I like to be with
my family and friends
at Christmas.

Cut out the strips opposite to make into paper chains.

WHAT SHALL I BUY MY ~~FAMILY~~ kids FOR CHRISTMAS?

Emuylite w Gray
Benthna teday inde
Tames Munay

mumandad mew   adJ Lds

On the First Day of Christmas...

Morning:

_____
_____
_____
_____
_____
_____

Afternoon:

_____
_____
_____
_____
_____
_____

Evening:

_____
_____
_____
_____
_____

What presents did you buy today?

lit up guira

Glue here and stick to opposite page.

Cut along
the solid
lines only.

Stop at
the dots.

Fold back along
the dotted lines
on the reverse
side of this page.

What are your favourite Christmas songs?

Jingle Bells

Ru...lf

We wish you a ...

On the Second Day of Christmas...

Morning:

_____
_____
_____
_____
_____
_____

Afternoon:

_____
_____
_____
_____
_____
_____

Evening:

_____
_____
_____
_____
_____

make a christmas wish list ...

Make a pretty pocket

← Cut along the dotted line
and discard this piece.

Cut along the dotted line
and discard this piece.

Glue here and stick to opposite page.

Glue here and stick to opposite page.

FUNNY FACE

Cut out these fancy
dress accessories and
stick them on photos of
you and your friends.

colour me beautiful...

The Snow Lay Deep and Crisp...

Can you spot a reindeer, a penguin, an owl and two birds chatting?

THINGS I LIKE to eat
at CHRISTMAS...

Stufing canclay
cany ponder cake

Make Your Own Place Name Cards

Cut along solid lines and fold along dashed lines.

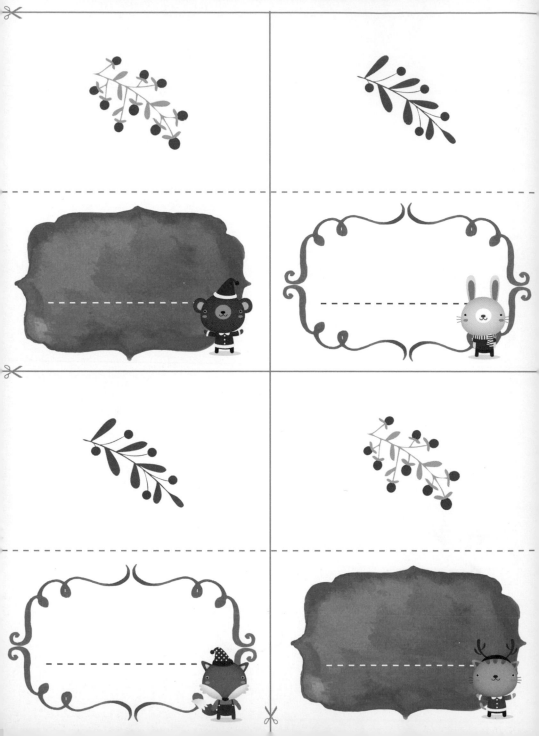

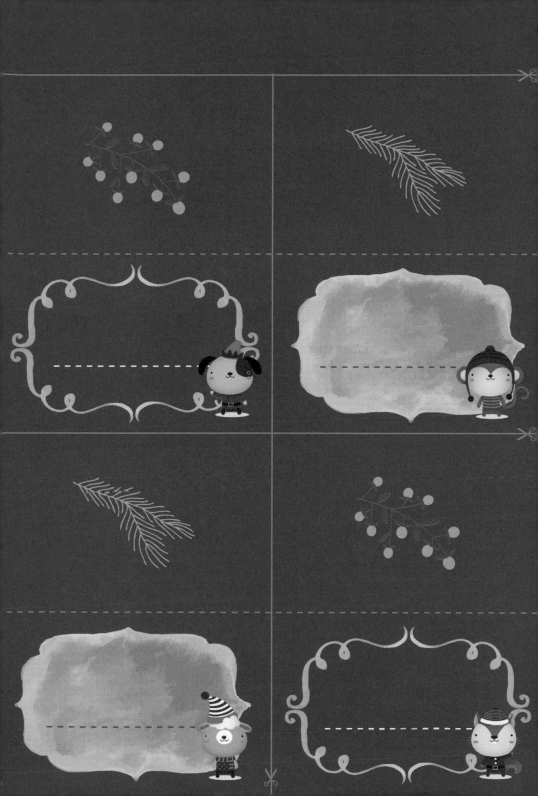

DRAW SOME HATS AND BEARDS ON THESE SANTAS.

Things I can see at Christmas...

on the third day of christmas...

Morning:

Afternoon:

Evening:

Write a letter to
Father Christmas. ---->

Hello!

hand gars
oo Bas
i pohe

colour me beautiful...

ISLA

✓

CLass

Write a poem about Christmas.

Not to
see fame

On the fourth day of Christmas...

Morning:

_____
_____
_____
_____
_____
_____

Afternoon:

_____
_____
_____
_____
_____
_____

Evening:

_____
_____
_____
_____
_____
_____

Photo

Make a list of all the people you have seen this christmas...

mum, cusins
dad gran

Write a thank you
note to someone you
care about. ------>

Thank you

Draw some angels.

Glue here and stick to opposite page.

Cut along the solid lines only. Stop at the dots.

Fold back along the dotted lines on the reverse side of this page.

Cut out the strips opposite to make into paper chains.

On the FiFth Day OF ChriStMaS...

Morning:

_____
_____
_____
_____
_____
_____

Afternoon:

_____
_____
_____
_____
_____
_____

Evening:

_____
_____
_____
_____
_____

Write or stick some cracker jokes here.

Cut out this
circle to create
a photo frame.

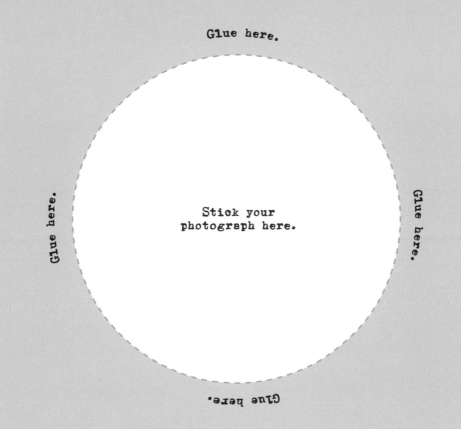

Glue here.

Glue here.

Glue here.

Stick your
photograph here.

Glue here.

On the Sixth Day of Christmas...

Morning:

_____
_____
_____
_____
_____
_____
_____

Afternoon:

_____
_____
_____
_____
_____
_____
_____

Evening:

_____
_____
_____
_____
_____
_____

Cut out these gift labels for your presents.

To _____

From _____

To _____

From _____

To _____

From _____

To _____

From _____

To _____

From _____

To _____

From _____

To _____

From _____

To _____

From _____

To _____

From _____

To _____

From _____

To _____

From _____

To _____

From _____

Cut along the
solid lines where
shown, then fold
the snowflake in
half along the
dotted line.

MAY ALL YOUR WISHES
COME TRUE...

Cut out the strips opposite to make into paper chains.

Can you find?

Father Christmas, an elf, a gingerbread man, a snowman, a reindeer and a fairy.

DRAW a CHRISTMAS STOCKING...

On the seventh day of christmas...

Morning:

Afternoon:

Evening:

SPOT FIVE DIFFERENCES.

Notes....

EMily
Bethnay

Cut out these gift labels for your presents.

On the EIGHTH Day Of Christmas...

Morning:

_____
_____
_____
_____
_____
_____

Afternoon:

_____
_____
_____
_____
_____
_____

Evening:

_____
_____
_____
_____
_____

Notes . . .

Make a Pretty Pocket

← Cut along the dotted line
and discard this piece.

Cut along the dotted line
and discard this piece.

Glue here and stick to opposite page.

Glue here and stick to opposite page.

Cut out these
decorations and
stick onto card
to make into
decorations to
hang on your tree.

places to visit at christmas...

Edinbra
ashada
Bzmr

STICK YOUR FAVOURITE
CHRISTMAS CARDS HERE.

On the NINth Day Of Christmas...

Morning:

Afternoon:

Evening:

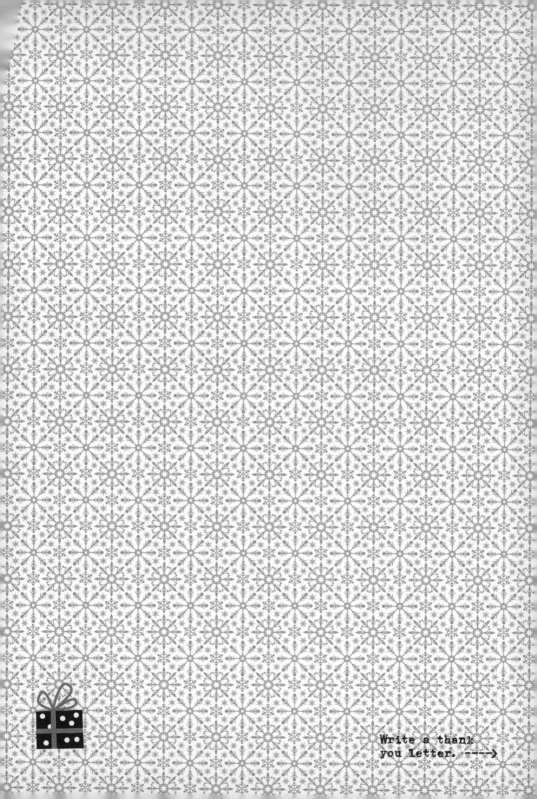

Write a thank
you letter. ---->

THANK YOU!

Cut out these pages to use as wrapping paper for small gifts.

On the tenth Day Of CHRISTMAS...

Morning:

_____
_____
_____
_____
_____
_____
_____

Afternoon:

_____
_____
_____
_____
_____
_____
_____

Evening:

_____
_____
_____
_____
_____
_____

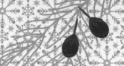

Write a poem about snow here.

ICE CREAM PACK

Write a thank you note to someone you care about. ------>

THANK YOU

Oh Christmas Tree!

Cut out the decorations below and decorate the tree opposite.

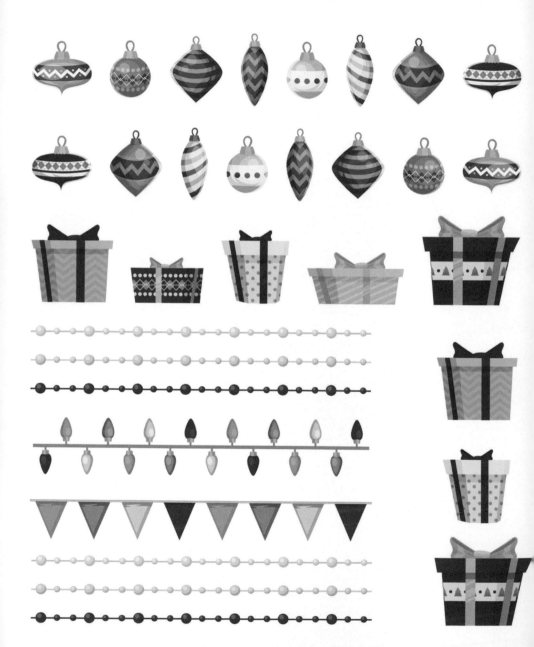

Create some tasty menus for a party.

STARTER:

MAIN COURSE:

DESSERT:

STARTER:

MAIN COURSE:

DESSERT:

STARTER:

MAIN COURSE:

DESSERT:

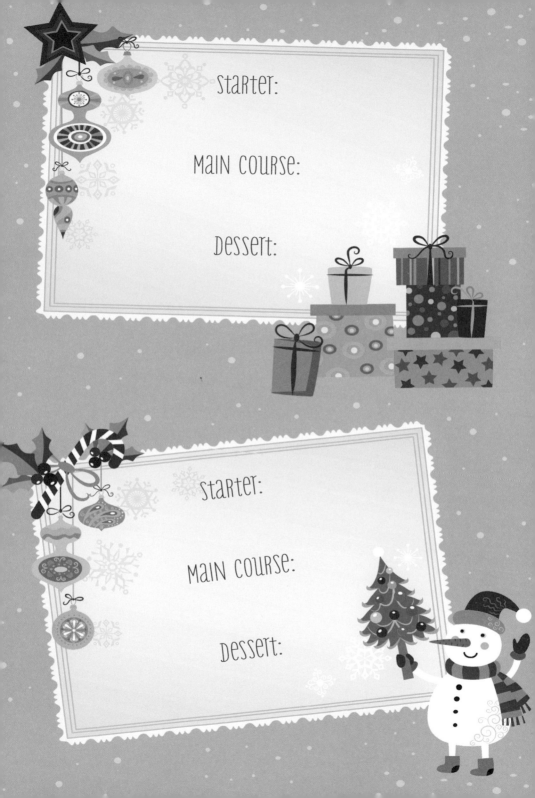

STARTER:

MAIN COURSE:

DESSERT:

Cut out the strips opposite to make into paper chains.

On the eleventh day of christmas...

Morning:

_____
_____
_____
_____
_____
_____
_____

Afternoon:

_____
_____
_____
_____
_____
_____
_____
_____

Evening:

_____
_____
_____
_____
_____
_____

Write down the
addresses of
the people you
want to send
Christmas
cards to.

ADDRESSES:

On the TWELFTH Day of Christmas...

Morning:

_____
_____
_____
_____
_____
_____
_____

Afternoon:

_____
_____
_____
_____
_____
_____
_____

Evening:

_____
_____
_____
_____
_____

MERRY CHRISTMAS!